THE LAST DAYS OF STEAM IN
DORSET
AND BOURNEMOUTH

'Merchant Navy' class No. 35019 *French Line CGT* arrives at Bournemouth Central with the Down 'Bournemouth Belle' on 25 May 1957. The 'Belle' was one of the famous named trains of the Southern. The 'Merchant Navies' also worked the 'Royal Wessex', 'Golden Arrow' and 'Atlantic Coast Express'. The 'Bournemouth Belle' was steam-hauled for the last time on 31 December 1966. Brush type 4 diesels took over this duty until the 'Belle' was withdrawn following electrification of the line in the summer of 1967.

Roy Panting

THE LAST DAYS OF STEAM IN
DORSET
AND BOURNEMOUTH

– DAVID HAYSOM AND JULIEN PARKER –

David Haysom   *Julien Parker*

*from
Pete, Mary and Stuart
Christmas '93*

ALAN SUTTON

First published in the United Kingdom in 1993
Alan Sutton Publishing Ltd · Phoenix Mill · Stroud · Gloucestershire

First published in the United States of America in 1993
Alan Sutton Publishing Inc · 83 Washington Street · Dover · NH 03820

British Library Cataloguing in Publication Data

Haysom, David
The Last Days of Steam in Dorset and Bournemouth
I. Title II. Julien Parker
385.09423

ISBN 0-7509-0108-2

Library of Congress Cataloging in Publication Data

Haysom, David.
    The Last Days of Steam in Dorset & Bournemouth / David Haysom & Julien Parker
        p. cm
    ISBN 0-7509-0180-2 : $26.00
    1. Railroads—England—Dorset. 2. Railroads—England—Bournemouth Region.   I.
Parker, Julien.   II. Title
TF58. D67H39 1993
625. 2′ 61′ 0942338—dc20
                                                                            92-44243
                                                                            CIP

Endpapers, Front: 'Battle of Britain' class No. 34073 249 Squadron heads the 12.35 p.m., Saturdays only, Waterloo–Weymouth train over Towngate level crossing into Poole station on 24 August 1963 (Roy Panting); back: 'Battle of Britain' class No. 34063 229 Squadron leaves Wimborne in 1963 with a Bournemouth West–Salisbury train (Stan Symes).

Typeset in 9/10 Palatino.
Typesetting and origination by
Alan Sutton Publishing Limited.
Printed and bound in Great Britain by
Butler & Tanner Ltd, Frome and London

Introduction

The majority of the photographs chosen for this book reflect the final years of steam in the 1960s. However, we have also covered the period from Nationalization to include some of the older locomotive classes which had been withdrawn during the gradual decline of steam. On the main Bournemouth–Weymouth line, the London and South Western and later Southern classes, including T9s, 'King Arthurs' and Moguls had given way to the Bulleid Pacifics and BR Standard classes. However, the last push-pull fitted M7s based at Bournemouth maintained services on the Swanage and Lymington branches until 1964. Dieselization of the Western Region was completed in 1965, although steam on the Southern Region survived until July 1967 when the Bournemouth–Waterloo line was electrified.

During the run-up to the withdrawal of steam the locomotives became increasingly neglected, and their nameplates and smokebox numbers were removed to deter the less scrupulous railway enthusiasts. Yet despite the grimy condition of the locomotives the crews on the Southern still achieved creditable running until the end.

The Nationalization of the railways from 1 January 1948 had seen the formation of the Southern Region from the former Southern Railway, while the Great Western Railway became the Western Region. The Somerset and Dorset also became part of the Southern Region. From April 1950 all Western Region lines in Dorset were transferred to the Southern regardless of operational considerations. Further changes came in 1962 when the main line west of Salisbury and the Somerset and Dorset from Blandford northwards were transferred to the Western Region. The initial effect of Nationalization on the railways of Dorset appeared minimal. However, the change in social and economic conditions after the Second World War plus a new pattern of transport requirements soon began to affect the railway network of Britain. The railways had been severely strained by wartime requirements and due to many outmoded traditions were not easily adaptable to change. The rapidly increasing road competition and lack of railway investment would soon force the inevitable contraction of the railway network.

In Dorset the Abbotsbury branch and the line to Portland and Easton both closed to passenger traffic in 1952 and foreshadowed the shape of things to come. Bus competition in both instances hastened the end of these lines. The long-term programme of modernization put forward by the Transport Commission in 1955 had little effect on Dorset's railways. However, additional platforms at Weymouth were added during 1956/57 and two years later DMUs were introduced on Weymouth–Bristol services. This resulted in the replacement of wooden platforms at Cattistock and Bradford Peverell & Stratton halts with precast concrete. The late 1950s also saw the closure of a number of small halts, including Corfe Mullen, Stourpaine & Durweston, Upwey Wishing Well and Monkton & Came. In 1960 goods traffic was withdrawn from Toller and Poole Quay, followed by Powerstock and Grimstone & Frampton in 1961, and Upwey and West Bay in 1962.

The Beeching Plan was published in March 1963 and recommended the development of potentially profitable routes but the closure of many other lines. In Dorset the West Moors–Salisbury line and the 'old road' from Brockenhurst to Hamworthy via Wimborne were the first to be closed during 1964. The following year saw the closure of the Lyme Regis branch, and the withdrawal of freight services from many of the smaller stations in the county as a result of centralization. However, the most controversial closure would be the Somerset and Dorset. Through trains, notably the 'Pines Express', had already been diverted to other routes from 1962. The line was progressively run down and despite strong opposition eventually closed on 7 March 1966. Under the Beeching Plan the Bridport branch was also scheduled for closure but was in fact to survive until 1975.

The Swanage branch was not mentioned in the Beeching proposals but came under threat from 1967. Local opposition forestalled final closure and we both witnessed the departure of the last train on 1 January 1972. However, unlike other branch lines in Dorset, this was not the end of the story, and through the determined efforts of the Swanage Railway Project steam still lives on at Swanage. The final section of this book is largely based on the work of one local photographer, Chris Phillips, whose photographs of Swanage in the 1960s capture everyday life at a branch-line station, now sadly only a memory.

Many aspects of railway life and practice have completely disappeared. Gone are the familiar scenes associated with pick-up goods trains, local branch services and steam sheds. Even locomotive-hauled trains are rapidly becoming extinct in this part of the country. Likewise, many interesting Victorian station buildings have been rendered obsolete under 'modernization', to be replaced by the vandal-resistant 'bus shelter' style of architecture. Many immaculately kept signal-boxes have also fallen victim to rationalization and the spread of colour-light signalling.

Thanks to the tireless efforts of railway photographers of the 1950s and '60s, memories of this twilight period of steam operation in Dorset have been captured on film for all to enjoy. With this in mind and in recognition of their efforts we gratefully acknowledge the help of: Ivan Beale, Colin Caddy, Richard Casserley, Keith Hastie, Ken MacDonald, Roy Panting, Chris Phillips, Stan Symes, Tony Trood and Allen White. Special thanks for their assistance are also due to Gerry Beale, Ernie Farwell, Alan Greatbatch, Bryan Green, Sarah Haysom, Jimmy Hunt, Bob Inman, Bob Richards, John Rutherford, Daniel Smith, Stan Smith, Richard de Peyer, curator of the Dorset County Museum, David Wilkinson of Weymouth Library, Lens of Sutton and the Tithe Barn Museum, Swanage.

We hope our choice of photographs evokes memories of the steam era, which can still be enjoyed on the Swanage Railway.

David Haysom and Julien Parker

THE LAST DAYS OF STEAM IN

DORSET

AND BOURNEMOUTH

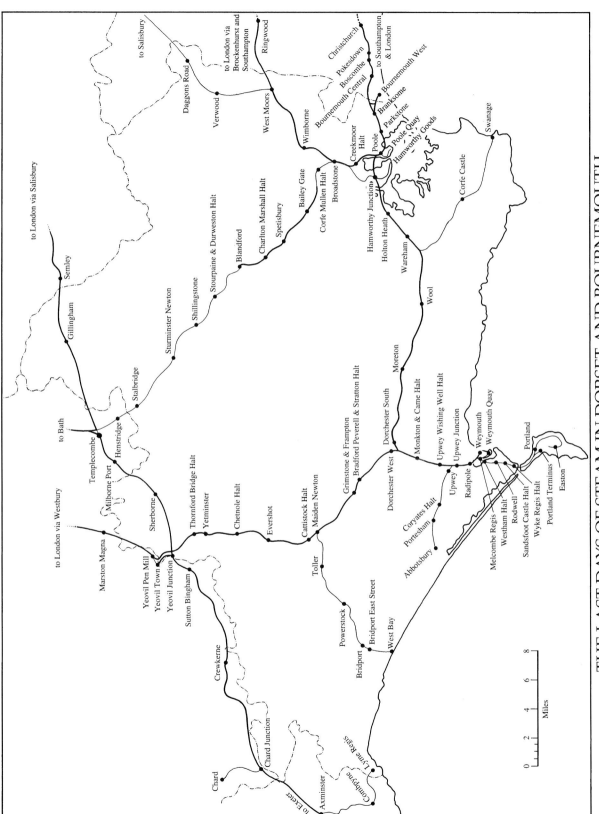

THE LAST DAYS OF STEAM IN DORSET AND BOURNEMOUTH

A fine study of No. 30850 *Lord Nelson* departing from Bournemouth Central with the 11.16 a.m. Bournemouth West–Newcastle train on 23 September 1961. This locomotive was the first of a class of sixteen designed by Maunsell. The 'King Arthurs' had proved an instant success but a more powerful class was needed to cope with the proposed 500 ton Continental expresses on the South Eastern routes such as Victoria to Dover. Initially only one locomotive, No. 850 *Lord Nelson*, was built at Eastleigh and completed in 1926. Another fifteen followed but they did not prove popular with loco crews due to firing difficulties. After modifications by Bulleid, including larger capacity tenders, the 'Nelsons' were fully employed during the early 1950s due to the unreliability of the new streamlined 'Merchant Navies'. After the 'Merchant Navies' and the majority of 'West Countries' had been rebuilt with conventional valve gear, the 'Lord Nelsons' were generally relegated from main-line duties. Withdrawal of the class took place during 1961/2, but happily this locomotive was preserved and can be seen occasionally hauling main-line steam specials.

Roy Panting

No. 6950 *Kingthorpe Hall* emerges from the short tunnel under Holdenhurst Road on an excursion from Malvern on 7 June 1958. The 'Halls' were designed by Collett and built between 1928 and 1950. The class largely survived until the 1960s, although all had been withdrawn by the end of 1965 with the dieselization of the whole of the Western Region.

Roy Panting

An overall view of Bournemouth Central with rebuilt 'West Country' class No. 34005 *Barnstaple* departing on a Weymouth–Waterloo service.

Chris Phillips

Bournemouth Central was host to a variety of interesting motive power during the 1950s. Brighton Atlantic No. 32422 *North Foreland* is seen with the 1.50 p.m. Bournemouth West–Brighton service on 7 July 1956. Shortly after this photograph was taken No. 32422 was restricted to light duties until it failed with a broken left cylinder when about to work a Ramblers special from East Croydon to Marlow. She was condemned with No. 32425 *Trevose Head* in September 1956. The remaining member of the class, No. 32424 *Beachy Head*, was withdrawn after a creditable performance on the 'Sussex Coast Limited' railtour of 13 April 1958.

Roy Panting

Another interesting visitor was Wainwright L class No. 31776, seen here on 25 May 1957. This was one of ten members of the class built for the SECR in Germany by Borsig of Berlin in 1914, shortly before the outbreak of the First World War. No. 31776 was based at Brighton from 1956 to assist with reorganized services to Tonbridge. This engine and her sisters, Nos 31777 and 31778, appeared occasionally at Bournemouth and Salisbury on through trains. No. 31776 was withdrawn in February 1961 and the final members of the class in December of that year.

Roy Panting

More Great Western steam at Bournemouth with Collett 0–6–0 No. 2230 on the 7.32 p.m. stopping service to Eastleigh on 13 August 1960. This class, built between 1930 and 1948, had been withdrawn by the end of 1965. However, No. 3205 has been preserved.

Roy Panting

Adams 02 class No. 30212 acts as station pilot on 5 September 1953. This successful class of tank engines built in the 1890s was the mainstay of the Isle of Wight lines from the 1920s until the end of steam on the island in 1966. The island engines carried names in addition to numbers and No. 24 *Calbourne* is now preserved on the Isle of Wight Steam Railway at Havenstreet.

Roy Panting

'King Arthur' class No. 30742 *Camelot* stands at Bournemouth with a service from Weymouth on 25 September 1954.

Roy Panting

No. 34090 *Sir Eustace Missenden Southern Railway* about to depart with the 5.05 p.m. Bournemouth West–Waterloo semi-fast on 20 August 1960. This locomotive, which had just been rebuilt, was officially a member of the 'Battle of Britain' class but was named after a former general manager of the Southern Railway. No. 34090 survived until the end of steam and was withdrawn from Eastleigh in July 1967.

Roy Panting

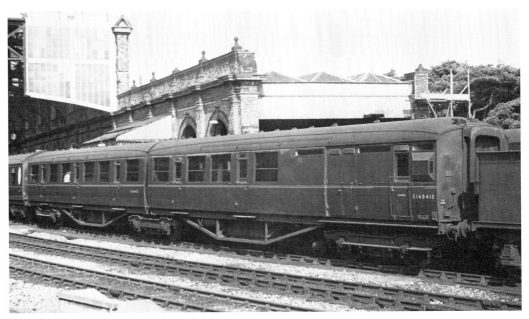

An unusual sight at Bournemouth on 20 August 1960 was a Gresley articulated set in a Poole–Bradford through train.

Roy Panting

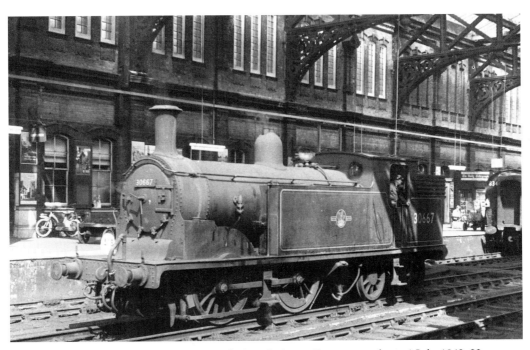

Push–pull fitted M7 class No. 30667 on piloting duties at Bournemouth on 4 July 1963. However, this engine was not exactly what it appeared. It had originally been No. 30106 and was renumbered No. 30667 in March 1961. The real No. 30667 was an unfitted short-framed engine which had in fact been withdrawn in November 1960 and scrapped as No. 30106 in February 1961. The replacement No. 30667, seen here, was one of the last of the class to be withdrawn in May 1964.

R.M. Casserley

An interesting view towards the end of the steam era as No. 34047 *Callington*, minus nameplates, stands at platform 3 with an Up train. A group of train spotters can be seen to the left of the locomotive which was withdrawn in 1967.

Chris Phillips

BR Standard class 4 No. 76008 arrives with a service from Weymouth shortly before this Bournemouth-based engine was withdrawn in May 1967. The two through lines seen in the previous photographs had been removed by the end of 1966.

Chris Phillips

The old and the new. BR Standard class 4 No. 75074 waits in the Down platform with a Waterloo–Weymouth service, while Crompton No. D6544 is seen in the original green livery at the Up platform. For many young train spotters the attraction of collecting engine numbers ended with the withdrawal of steam. The common practice of removing nameplates and smokebox numbers was intended to deter the less scrupulous railway enthusiast.

Chris Phillips

A general view of the Down platform in the mid-1960s before the addition of the concrete foot-bridge. Although this book is devoted to the locomotives and staff, this view of the passengers reminds us that fashions have also changed.

Chris Phillips

Another view in the final months of steam shows 'West Country' class No. 34001 *Exeter* arriving at the Up platform. The nameplates on this engine have been removed, although the number has been painted on the smokebox door. In the Down platform an electro-diesel is attracting the interest of the young train spotters. The 'third rail' pending electrification can be clearly seen on the right.

Chris Phillips

In earlier days the crew of 'Modified Hall' class No. 6969 *Wraysbury Hall* peer from the cab on 18 June 1960. This locomotive was withdrawn in February 1965.

Roy Panting

'West Country' class No. 34013 *Okehampton* leaving Bournemouth with a Weymouth service, attracts the interest of photographers whose efforts have made this book possible.

Chris Phillips

The last days of steam at Bournemouth, with 'Merchant Navy' class No. 35007 *Aberdeen Commonwealth* at the Down platform with a Weymouth service. On the far left is a Crompton in the original green livery, while a similar engine can be seen in the centre in the brand-new blue livery.

Chris Phillips

A general view of Bournemouth shed from the Down platform on 3 June 1962. The shed closed with the end of steam on the Southern Region in July 1967 and the area has now become part of the station car park, of which the base of the brick-built shed forms the edge. Nearest the camera is push–pull fitted M7 class No. 30108, a regular on the Swanage branch, while on shed is a variety of motive power, including a rebuilt 'West Country', Standard class 5 and several M7 tanks.

David Haysom Collection

The shape of things to come. A Crompton diesel in the new blue and yellow livery is seen alongside 'West Country' class No. 34024 *Tamar Valley* and BR Standard class 4 No. 76009 on 27 March 1967. Ironically, the Cromptons, or class 33s to the younger enthusiasts, have now been ousted by the Wessex Electrics on the main Waterloo–Weymouth line. However, a number of the Cromptons remain operational at the time of writing and others are scheduled for preservation.

Roy Panting

Before and after. The top picture shows streamlined 'Merchant Navy' class No. 35005 *Canadian Pacific* at Bournemouth shed on 16 February 1957. All members of the class were rebuilt between 1956 and 1959 with conventional valve gear and the streamlined casing removed, mainly due to the difficulties with maintenance. This locomotive was rebuilt in June 1959 and withdrawn from Weymouth shed in October 1965. However, she was fortunate in being sent to Woodham's yard at Barry, from where she was purchased in 1973 and is now preserved on the Great Central Railway.

Roy Panting

The appearance of the arguably more attractive rebuilt 'Merchant Navies' is seen to good effect in this view of No. 35022 *Holland–America Line* at Bournemouth on 5 November 1960. In their rebuilt form the 'Merchants' gave good performances on express services from Waterloo to Salisbury and Waterloo to Weymouth until the end of steam. No. 35022 has also been preserved and is undergoing restoration at Swanage. Of the 'Merchant Navies' preserved, Nos 35028 *Clan Line* and 35027 *Port Line* have often been seen on main-line steam specials.

Roy Panting

Nicely turned out Drummond M7 class No. 30060 provides an interesting contrast to the 'Merchant Navy' class seen on the previous page. The M7s were designed at the end of the Victorian era yet were still providing good service in the early 1960s, while the 'Merchants' were a mere twenty years old. Both classes would shortly be withdrawn with the deliberate policy of ending steam on Britain's railways. No. 30060, seen here on 14 April 1960, was built at Nine Elms in December 1905 and became one of the thirty long-framed members of the class to be fitted for push–pull working in 1930. This is denoted by the distinctive Westinghouse pump on the right-hand side of the smokebox. Apart from No. 126, which had been experimentally superheated in 1926, and No. 672, all locomotives in the class entered BR service and No. 30060 was withdrawn in July 1961. Although the last withdrawals took place in May 1964, two of the class have been preserved – No. 30245 in the National Collection and No. 30053 on the Swanage Railway. Upon withdrawal No. 30053 had a recorded mileage of 1,786,577. However, she was overhauled at Eastleigh and shipped to the United States to become a static exhibit at Steamtown Vermont until repatriation in 1987.

Roy Panting

A driver's view of Bournemouth shed in 1966, showing 'West Country' class No. 34006 *Bude*. These air-smoothed Pacifics were plagued by drifting exhaust which obscured forward vision. The original short deflectors were often extended and this locomotive is an extreme example of the practice.

Stan Symes

The 'Britannias' were built at Derby and introduced in 1951. They were numbered 70000–54, with the final two being built in 1954. Many of the class were named after poets, while Nos 70014–29 perpetuated the names of famous Great Western engines of the past. The last five locomotives, originally allocated to Scotland, carried names of Scottish Firths. Seen here on 10 July 1954 is No. 70014 *Iron Duke*. The prototype engine, No. 70000 *Britannia*, became part of the National Collection upon withdrawal, while the last survivor, No. 70013 *Oliver Cromwell*, withdrawn in 1968, has also been preserved.

Roy Panting

Urie S15 class No. 30504 enters the shed yard on 4 September 1954. The original class of twenty locomotives were built at Eastleigh during 1920 and 1921. A further twenty-five were built by Maunsell between 1927 and 1936 with various modifications. These were generally considered more successful than the original series. In 1935/36 No. 30504 and six other members of the class had their Urie 5,000 gallon tenders replaced with Drummond-pattern 4,000 gallon tenders from withdrawn C8 class 4-4-0s. No. 30504 is seen here before the Drummond tender was replaced in May 1958 with a Urie tender from a withdrawn H15. This engine and No. 30505 were the first members of the class to be withdrawn in November 1962. Nos 30499 and 30506 have been preserved.

Roy Panting

Adams B4 class No. 30093 seen in the shed yard on 22 July 1956. Originally one of a class of twenty-five engines, No. 93 was built at Nine Elms in 1892 and worked at Southampton Docks, carrying the name *St Malo*. She was transferred to Bournemouth shed upon arrival of the ex-WD USA tanks in 1947. Following Nationalization this locomotive was repainted in unlined black livery in September 1952 and renumbered 30093. As the engine was no longer engaged at Southampton Docks, the name *St Malo* was omitted in the repaint. During the 1950s No. 30093 worked the line to Poole Quay until its closure in 1960, when the engine was withdrawn. No. 30096, formerly *Normandy*, and No. 30102 *Granville* have been preserved.

Roy Panting

This useful photograph for modellers shows Drummond 700 class No. 30690 at Bournemouth on 14 February 1960. Even the 71B Bournemouth shed plate can be seen clearly on the smokebox door. This class of thirty locomotives was built in 1897. From the early days they were known to their crews as 'Black Motors'. The class was extensively rebuilt by Urie and they continued to provide good service for over sixty years, especially during the Second World War. Withdrawal began in 1957 and No. 30690 was one of the last to be officially withdrawn in December 1962. However, owing to the 'Big Freeze' of 1962/3, several members of the class were resurrected to perform snow clearance work.

Roy Panting

Bulleid's most austere design was the purely functional Q1 class. The forty members of the class were built to meet the demands for powerful goods engines during the Second World War. However, their efficient performance made up for their looks, although crews often found braking rather testing. This view shows No. 33020 at Bournemouth shed on 20 August 1955. Note the original 'lion on the wheel' emblem, replaced on all repaints after 1958 with a generally more pleasing design, subject to the availability of transfers. The first locomotive of the class, No. 33001, built at Brighton works in March 1942, is now preserved on the Bluebell Railway.

Roy Panting

Two studies of the turntable at Bournemouth allow comparison of the unrebuilt and rebuilt 'West Country'/'Battle of Britain' classes. Unrebuilt 'West Country' class No. 34004 *Yeovil* is seen here on 29 April 1956. This locomotive was rebuilt in March 1958 and withdrawn in July 1967.

Roy Panting

'Battle of Britain' class No. 34050 *Royal Observer Corps* was rebuilt in August 1958 and is seen on 2 July 1961 after working a special excursion from Waterloo carrying members of the ROC and their friends. At a special ceremony at Waterloo on that day, No. 34050 was entitled to a long-service medal, having been in traffic for twelve years. The appropriately coloured plaque can be seen on the cabside.

Roy Panting

BR Standard class 5 No. 73089 *Maid of Astolat* at Bournemouth shed turntable on 5 April 1963. The 70A Nine Elms shed plate can be clearly seen in this detailed view. No. 73089 was transferred to Eastleigh (70D) in September 1964 and then to Guildford (70C) in October 1965, where she remained until withdrawal in September 1966.

Roy Panting

'Merchant Navy' class No. 35029 *Ellerman Lines* enters the shed yard on 7 April 1963. This locomotive, built at Eastleigh in February 1949, was the penultimate member of the class. No. 35029 went new to Bournemouth together with other 'Merchant Navies' to replace the 'Lord Nelsons' on the express services to London. However, in September of the same year they were transferred to Dover to replace 'Battle of Britain' class locomotives on the Continental expresses. In 1950 No. 35029 was derailed at London Bridge station and caused chaos as many evening rush-hour services had to be cancelled. *Ellerman Lines* was officially named at Southampton Docks on 1 March 1951. The same year, painted in the unsuccessful BR blue livery, it hauled a royal special, carrying the King and Queen of Denmark from Dover Marine to Victoria. After rebuilding in September 1959, No. 35029 remained at Nine Elms until 1964, when she was transferred to Weymouth due to increasing dieselization. *Ellerman Lines* was withdrawn in September 1966, and although preserved at the National Railway Museum in York, she is displayed in a sectioned condition.

Roy Panting

U class No. 31800 with the 3.33 p.m. empty stock working from Southampton on 29 June 1963. No. 31800 was originally built in 1926 as a tank engine by Maunsell as part of the K class, which were named after rivers. However, this locomotive, as No. A800 *River Cray*, was involved in a derailment at Sevenoaks in August 1927. It was decided to rebuild the class and those still under construction as 2–6–0 tender engines. Due to adverse publicity in the national press, the river names were also omitted. Equally adept at passenger or freight work, the class performed well until withdrawal which commenced in 1963.

Roy Panting

'Merchant Navy' class No. 35014 *Nederland Line* is shown with the Down 'Bournemouth Belle' on 14 February 1960, while BR Standard class 4 No. 75066 waits in the main platform with a stopping service to Weymouth.

Roy Panting

BR Standard class 5 No. 73110 *The Red Knight* leaves Bournemouth with the 12.35 p.m. relief Waterloo–Weymouth train on 14 April 1960.

Roy Panting

Q class No. 30541 passes Bournemouth shed with a Holton Heath workers' train to Christchurch on 14 April 1960.

Roy Panting

A general view of Bournemouth West on 14 July 1960, with 'King Arthur' class No. 30790 *Sir Villiars* and an unidentified push-pull fitted M7. The fine array of LSWR lattice signals is also seen to good effect. A station on this site originally opened in 1874 as the terminus of the extension of the LSWR line from Poole. The station formed the southern terminus of the Somerset and Dorset Railway until the final months of operation in 1965. Passenger services to Bournemouth West ceased in October 1965. The terminus was later demolished and the land has now become part of the Wessex Way relief road.

H.C. Casserley

M7 class No. 30108 at Bournemouth West on 6 April 1963 with a Brockenhurst local train. No. 30108 was a regular sight on the Swanage branch and became one of the last members of the class to be withdrawn in May 1964.

Roy Panting

BR Standard class 5 No. 73054 with the 5.30 p.m. Bournemouth West–Templecombe service on 23 June 1962. Twenty members of this class were given Arthurian names following withdrawal of the 'King Arthur' class.

Roy Panting

A fine study of Maunsell U class No. 31619 at Bournemouth West with the 6.40 p.m. Woking train on 7 June 1965. This service was regularly worked by a Guildford-based engine, hence the 70C shed code chalked on the smokebox door. No. 31619 was withdrawn six months later.

Roy Panting

BR Standard class 4 No. 76026 prepares to depart with the 6.40 p.m. Bath train on 29 June 1963. Maunsell set No. 616 on the right had previously been allocated to London central district on conversion for push–pull working in 1960. This set was withdrawn in October 1964.

Roy Panting

BR Standard class 9F No. 92220 *Evening Star* departs from Bournemouth West on 8 September 1962 with the last 'Pines Express' to Manchester over the Somerset and Dorset. Appropriately, *Evening Star* was the last steam locomotive built for British Railways in March 1960. Upon withdrawal in March 1965, after only five years in service, this engine was understandably preserved.

Roy Panting

Drummond T9 class No. 30702 enters Branksome with a Bournemouth West–Salisbury train on 21 August 1954. The former Branksome triangle was taken out of use in 1965, although the signal-box seen here survives at the junction to the sidings and carriage shed erected after the closure of Bournemouth West station.

H.C. Casserley

'Merchant Navy' class No. 35008 *Orient Line* passes Branksome with the 11.17 a.m. Weymouth–Waterloo express on 2 July 1966. Branksome station opened in 1893 and remains in use today, although the canopies seen here have been partially removed in recent years.

Roy Panting

Parkstone station on 6 July 1961, with S15 class No. 30840 in charge of a train for Weymouth. The main station building survives bereft of its large canopy, while the Down platform buildings have been replaced with a 'bus shelter'.

R.M. Casserley

BR Standard class 4 No. 75027 enters Parkstone station on 13 July 1962 with a train off the Somerset and Dorset comprised of Bulleid three-coach corridor set No. 968. These sets were allocated to the S&D in 1959 to replace the pre-war Maunsell sets. However, due to the pressure of summer services in 1960, they were needed on the main line and did not return to the S&D until the following year. The locomotive seen here is now preserved on the Bluebell Railway.

H.C. Casserley

BR Standard class 9F No. 92233 approaches Poole with the 10.35 a.m. Bournemouth West–Manchester train on 14 July 1962.

Roy Panting

Electro-diesel No. E6007 leaves Poole banking a Channel Islands boat train up Parkstone bank in the mid-1960s.

Chris Phillips

U class No. 31792 enters Poole with a Bournemouth West–Salisbury train on 7 July 1961. The two busy level crossings on the sharp curve outside the station must have been a nightmare for drivers of Down trains. The roof of Poole 'A' box is just visible in the distance. This box controlled the High Street crossing until 1977, although the associated foot-bridge of 1872 still survives today.

R.M. Casserley

Many will remember the old Poole station with its distinctive curved platforms. Push-pull fitted M7 class No. 30105 built in 1905 stands at the Up platform, shortly before withdrawal in May 1963. This station was replaced by a characterless concrete structure in 1971, which in turn was replaced by a purpose-built modern structure of unusual design in 1988.

Keith Hastie

27

More modern motive power at Poole as BR Standard 5 No. 73042 prepares to depart from the Up platform. The 71G Weymouth shed code, visible on the smokebox door, was changed to 70G in 1963. This locomotive remained at Weymouth shed until withdrawal in August 1965.

Keith Hastie

Bulleid Q1 class No. 33023 arrives at Poole with the 9.20 a.m. Swansea–New Milton train on 30 July 1960. The former Poole 'B' or West box seen in the distance still survives, but the large goods shed on the right has been demolished and the majority of the yard removed.

Roy Panting

BR Standard class 4 No. 76017 arrives at Poole with Bulleid set No. 793 on a Bournemouth West–Salisbury service. This locomotive was withdrawn in July 1965.

Keith Hastie

A general view, looking east, of the old station at Poole on 6 July 1961. The curved platforms are well illustrated, while just to the right of this picture was the tramway to Poole Quay, which had closed in May 1960. The track was lifted or covered over during 1961.

R.M. Casserley

Poole Quay on 15 July 1959, with Adams B4 class No. 30093 engaged in shunting duties. This line was last used on 30 April 1960 and officially closed two days later.

Roy Panting

Across the harbour at Hamworthy Quay was the Hamworthy Coal Co. wharf. Seen here on 6 September 1954 is 0–4–0 No. 2 *Western Pride*. Sister engine No. 1 *Bonnie Prince Charlie* is preserved at the Didcot Railway Centre.

Roy Panting

An interesting view at Poole on 23 August 1952 showing two members of the Drummond T9 class. No. 30287 is seen with an Eastleigh–Wimborne train, while No. 30728 stands in the goods yard. Both these locomotives had covered almost two million miles by withdrawal in 1961 and 1956 respectively. The sole survivor of the class, No. 30120, repainted in Southern livery, can currently be seen on the Swanage Railway.

Roy Panting

Midland 4F class No. 44560 leaves Poole yard with a Somerset and Dorset goods on 19 April 1964. This particular engine was one of those built for the S&D to a Midland design.

Roy Panting

'West Country' class No. 34031 *Torrington* leaves Poole with the 12.35 p.m. Waterloo–Weymouth service on 19 April 1964. To the left, Q class No. 30546 can be seen at the entrance to the goods yard.

Roy Panting

In contrast, Great Western Churchward 4300 class No. 5370 leaves Poole yard with a Dorchester goods on 6 August 1959.

Roy Panting

Maunsell U class No. 31816 is seen in charge of another Dorchester-bound goods on 30 April 1964. The lights of Poole speedway stadium can be seen in the distance.

Roy Panting

BR Standard class 3 tank No. 82029 leaves Poole with the 2.25 p.m. Bournemouth West–Brockenhurst train via the 'old road' on 19 April 1964.

Roy Panting

BR Standard class 5 No. 73093 departs from Hamworthy Junction with the 12.12 p.m. Weymouth–Bournemouth service on 10 June 1967. The Down loop leading to the Hamworthy Goods line can be seen on the left.

Alan Greatbatch Collection

A general view of Hamworthy Junction station on 14 October 1965. These buildings and the signal-box had replaced the original station in 1893, on completion of the Holes Bay curve. The Down platform buildings on the left were replaced by a 'bus shelter' in 1972, but the 59-lever signal-box survives to control the line to Hamworthy Goods.

J.H. Lucking/Dorset County Museum

A close-up of the LSWR co-acting starting signal as push–pull fitted M7 class No. 30057 approaches the Down platform with a Bournemouth Central–Weymouth service on 14 October 1959.

A.G. Thorpe/Alan Greatbatch Collection

A fine view of the LSWR lattice signal with co-acting arms at the junction of the line to Broadstone. This signal was replaced in December 1961 by an upper quadrant one of SR construction, as seen on page 34. The single line to Broadstone was closed on 4 May 1964 and the track later removed.

Alan Greatbatch Collection

Q1 class No. 33015 enters the Down loop at the junction station with a train for Hamworthy Goods.
Alan Greatbatch Collection

Hamworthy Junction station looking west, showing an unidentified Bulleid Q1 on the approach to the goods line. The locomotive shed in the distance had closed during May 1954. In its latter years the shed allocation had been two M7 and two B4 tanks.

Alan Greatbatch Collection

Stanier 'Black Five' No. 45493 seen at Hamworthy Junction in 1966 with a through service to the Midlands via Basingstoke and Reading.

Stan Symes

Hamworthy Goods looking towards the junction station on 14 July 1960, with BR Standard class 4 No. 76015 engaged on shunting duties. Despite continuing uncertainty this line remains in use.

H.C. Casserley

The Rail Enthusiasts' Club tour on 7 June 1958 visited the former Hamworthy station which had closed to passengers in 1896. The original station building had survived as goods offices.

R.M. Casserley

An unusual view of Hamworthy Goods, with BR Standard class 3 No. 77014 on the 'LCGB Dorset and Hants Tour' on 16 October 1966.

Roy Panting

BR Standard class 4 No. 76019 near Holton Heath with a goods train from Dorchester on 14 January 1960.

Roy Panting

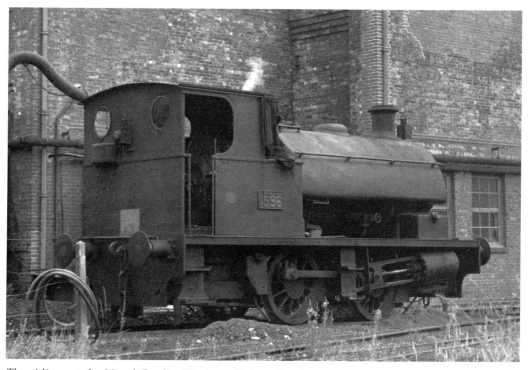

The sidings at the Naval Cordite Works at Holton Heath were worked by a Bagnall 0–4–0 saddle tank, No. 1596. This view was taken on 17 July 1959.

Roy Panting

Holton Heath station on 3 October 1960, with 'Battle of Britain' class No. 34053 *Sir Keith Park* running tender-first on the 12.53 p.m. Bournemouth Central–Weymouth stopping service.

Roy Panting

A wintry scene at Holton Heath on 14 January 1960, with 'King Arthur' class No. 30788 *Sir Urre of the Mount* on another stopping service from Bournemouth Central to Weymouth. Holton Heath opened in 1916 for use by workers at the Naval Cordite Works. General public use did not commence until 1924, and the station remains open today partly to serve the various industrial units which now occupy the old cordite factory site.

Roy Panting

Wareham signal-box and crossing in the mid-1960s. Two gates, one of LSWR origin (left) and one of Southern Railway origin, can be seen. Frequent damage occurred when cars failed to stop and this accounted for the variety in the gates. The box is still in BR use but the level crossing has been replaced by a flyover.

Chris Phillips

A fine interior view of Wareham box in 1966. The 30-lever Stevens-pattern frame, block instrument shelf and track diagram are in pristine condition. The duster on the signal lever was common and prevented the levers from rusting through contact with the signalman's hands.

Chris Phillips

Pushed by a Crompton diesel, 4TC set No. 419 makes its way over the level crossing towards Bournemouth in 1967. This was the shape of things to come and these sets soon ousted all regular steam working on the Bournemouth–Weymouth main line.

Chris Phillips

In contrast, Bulleid 'Battle of Britain' class No. 34064 *Fighter Command*, fitted with a Giesl oblong ejector, heads towards Wareham with a train for Weymouth. Prominent in the view is former crossing keeper's cottage No. 30, one of two which were later demolished.

Chris Phillips

Rebuilt 'West Country' class No. 34093 *Saunton* prepares to depart from Wareham with a Weymouth–Waterloo service. This locomotive survived until the final month of steam on the Southern Region in July 1967.

Chris Phillips

An unusual visitor to Wareham was this unidentified Great Western tender engine seen running light past the Up platform in the early 1960s.

Chris Phillips

A rare sight at Wareham on 15 August 1953. LMS diesel-electric locomotive No. 10000 on trials. This was the first main-line diesel locomotive in Britain, built at Derby in 1947. No. 10000 later returned to the Midland Region and until withdrawal was chiefly confined to fast freight work.

R.R. Bowler

'King Arthur' class No. 30770 *Sir Prianius* departs from Wareham with the 10.10 a.m. Weymouth–Bournemouth train on 7 July 1962.

Roy Panting

The fireman of BR Standard class 4 tank No. 80016 replenishes the tanks from the water column on the Up platform, on a stopping service to Bournemouth in the mid-1960s. The building on the right was formerly an inspector's office and was later demolished.

Chris Phillips

Crompton diesel No. D6512 and an unidentified BR Standard class 4 tank locomotive wait for permission to depart light engine to Bournemouth shed in the summer of 1965. Both locomotives had come off the Swanage branch. The diesel had worked down from Waterloo and berthed its stock, and the tank had been the shunting locomotive at Swanage. They were coupled together to save train movements.

Chris Phillips

Grimy BR Standard Mogul No. 76010 viewed at Wareham Up platform on the last day of scheduled steam working on the Swanage branch, 4 September 1966. Driver Bill Henstridge waits, prior to running round. Since the departure of the M7s all branch trains had used the Up platform for running-round purposes and the Up bay had fallen into disuse.

Chris Phillips

BR Standard class 4 tank No. 80134 prepares to run round the Swanage branch train. This manoeuvre caused severe delays to road traffic on the A351, as the positioning of the run-round points involved traversing the level crossing. The Up starting signal is in the off position and the gates are closed to road traffic.

Chris Phillips

In earlier days Drummond M7 class No. 30056 prepares to propel its Maunsell push-pull set onto the Down main line and back into the Down bay, in readiness for a return trip to Swanage. This photograph was taken during the summer of 1963 and the locomotive was withdrawn at the end of that year.

Chris Phillips

Stan Smith in the booking office at Wareham during the summer of 1966. Stan started in the goods office at Swanage in September 1953. However, he spent his first three nights at Wool to prevent the tickets being pinched by the painters who were redecorating the booking office! He later worked at Poole parcels in 1956 and the booking office at Wareham from 1957 until September 1966. After a brief spell in London he continued on relief duties until retirement in March 1990.

Chris Phillips

Seen in its last month of service, 'King Arthur' class No. 30782 *Sir Brian* heads a stopping train to Bournemouth into Wareham Up platform. This view was recorded in September 1962.

Chris Phillips

'West Country' class No. 34023 *Blackmore Vale* pauses at Wareham Down platform on a semi-fast service to Weymouth. This locomotive was a regular performer on the Bournemouth–Weymouth line in the mid-1960s.

Chris Phillips

In contrast to the previous photograph, 'Merchant Navy' class No. 35023 *Holland–Afrika Line*, with its nameplate missing, passes through Wareham with a Channel Island boat train bound for Waterloo. These locomotives were heavier than the 'West Country' class and were not permitted down the Swanage branch due to excessive axle loading. The neglected state of the locomotive was an unfortunate feature of the rundown of steam.

Chris Phillips

During the mid-1960s BR was looking for economies and this led to the demolition of the toilet block on the Up platform at Wareham. Staff members Bert Sampson and 'Paddy' Mulqueen seem oblivious to the notice on the chalked board! Note also the repainted canopy valance minus the ornamental beading strips. This was another unfortunate casualty of the time.

Chris Phillips

A pleasant view of Wareham looking east towards the level crossing gates. Shunter Bert Sampson has just coupled up Ivatt No. 41260 to its branch set, consisting of push-pull stock, following the run-round procedure. No. 41260, with driver Johnny Spicer, will then cross tracks to the Down main, before reversing back into the Down bay. This scene can be dated to the summer of 1964.

Chris Phillips

'West Country' class No. 34037 *Clovelly* passes Holme crossing. This ground frame was abolished on 21 April 1965 and automatic half-barriers brought into use. However, the crossing box at nearby East Stoke is surprisingly still manned due to dangerous road access.

Chris Phillips

The original station at Wool looking west on 12 August 1965. Wool opened in 1847 and remained largely unchanged until the main building was replaced by a purely functional concrete and glass structure in 1969. The small goods shed on the left still survives but the Down sidings were lifted in April 1988. These sidings had been largely retained for use by the Army in connection with nearby Bovington Camp, although the goods yard had closed for general traffic in June 1967.

J.H. Lucking/Dorset County Museum

An unusual visitor to Dorset during 1967, the final year of steam on the Southern Region, was A4 Pacific No. 4468 *Sir Nigel Gresley*, seen here approaching Moreton.

Chris Phillips

Moreton station on 23 September 1965. This view looking towards Dorchester was taken the same week the goods yard closed and six months after staffing ceased. The main buildings on the Up platform were demolished in recent years after unsuccessful attempts to let the property.

J.H. Lucking/Dorset County Museum

Rebuilt 'West Country' class No. 34004 *Yeovil* pauses at Moreton with a Weymouth–Bournemouth service during 1965.

Chris Phillips

A general view of the original Dorchester South station on 20 January 1956. This was intended as a through station to Exeter, but the completion of the route from Salisbury to Yeovil made this unnecessary. However, until 1970 Up trains had to reverse into the station. Note the SR bogie brake van on the right which was one of a batch of vans built as bogie coaches in 1925 and converted in 1934. Further purpose-built vans were also constructed. These bogie vans gave a better ride than the four-wheel types and in fact some remain in service today.

R.M. Casserley

'Merchant Navy' class No. 35011 *General Steam Navigation* prepares to depart from the Up platform at Dorchester South with the 11.30 a.m. Weymouth–Waterloo service on 11 June 1962. Although the new Up platform had been constructed in 1970, the main station building remained in use until 1987. A new Up building and waiting shelters similar in appearance to Dorchester West station were built as a joint venture by British Rail and brewers Eldridge Pope. This attractive new building shows that good station architecture is not entirely a thing of the past.

Roy Panting

A view of the Down platform on 4 September 1959, a few months after the unusual tall signal-box had been superseded by the modern brick-built alternative just visible in the distance. This new box was reduced to a ground frame in 1970 but resumed its former role when the box at Dorchester Junction was abolished in June 1985.

H.B. Priestley

'Battle of Britain' class No. 34077 *603 Squadron* runs light engine past the Down platform at Dorchester South. The new Up platform was built to the right of this photograph in 1970.

Chris Phillips

No. 5972 *Olton Hall* is seen between Bincombe North and South tunnels with a Weymouth goods in 1959.

I.D. Beale

'King Arthur' class No. 30773 *Sir Lavaine* and an unidentified 'Schools' work a ten-coach train up the bank from Weymouth past Upwey Wishing Well Halt in 1959.

I.D. Beale

Upwey & Broadwey station, seen here on 7 July 1961, was opened after completion of the Abbotsbury branch in 1885. Until closure of this line on 1 December 1952, this station was known as Upwey Junction, the branch platform being to the left of this view. Upwey remains open today, although all the original station buildings have given way to the purely functional 'bus shelter' style of architecture.

R.M. Casserley

Upwey & Broadwey signal-box, situated at the south end of the station, was closed on 1 March 1970. In latter years wooden panelling beneath the windows was replaced with the brickwork which can be seen in this view.

I.D. Beale

Radipole Halt opened in June 1905 and is seen here with the distinctive Great Western corrugated-iron pagoda waiting shelters. The halt was later rebuilt with concrete platforms, and the pagodas were replaced by 'bus shelters' in June 1977. However, due to doubts over safety, the halt was closed on 1 January 1984 and demolition quickly followed.

Lens of Sutton

An unidentified BR Standard leaves Weymouth with a goods train for Bournemouth Central. Weymouth shed can be seen in the distance.

Chris Phillips

Weymouth shed around 1965. The GWR engine shed had housed a few Southern locomotives from 1939, and in 1950 the line south from Dorchester was transferred to the Southern Region. Seen here are Stanier 'Black Five' No. 45240 and, under the wheel drop, BR Standard class 4 No. 76068. This locomotive was withdrawn from Eastleigh in October 1965. The shed closed with the end of steam in July 1967.

Colin Caddy

BR Standard class 4 No. 76008 comes off shed at Weymouth shortly before withdrawal in May 1967.

Chris Phillips

'West Country' class No. 34001 *Exeter* departs from Weymouth with a Waterloo service on 5 August 1963.

J.H. Lucking/Dorset County Museum

Ivatt No. 41298 with Bulleid five-coach set No. 847 on piloting duties at Weymouth during the summer of 1965. The end of set-working on the Southern Region came in March 1966, when the surviving Bulleid coaches remained 'loose' until withdrawal. The coaches forming set No. 847 lasted until July/August 1967, with the exception of corridor third No. 75, withdrawn in December 1965.

Chris Phillips

'Merchant Navy' class No. 35023 *Holland–Afrika Line* stands at the new platform 5 with a service from Waterloo. This locomotive worked the last steam-hauled Waterloo–Weymouth passenger train in 1967, which can be seen on page 62.

Chris Phillips

One of the new three-car DMUs is seen in platform 6 during trials to Weymouth on 17 February 1959.

J.H. Lucking/Dorset County Museum

Great Western and Southern steam meet at Weymouth. The crew of No. 6926 *Holkham Hall* watch 'West Country' class No. 34010 *Sidmouth* preparing to depart with a Bournemouth Central service. Both engines were withdrawn in 1965 but No. 34010, after languishing at Barry for many years, has now been sold for preservation.

Chris Phillips

Two BR Standard class 5s, Nos 73042 and 73080 *Merlin*, prepare to haul the 6.30 p.m. Weymouth to Bournemouth Central service. Half of this train comprised parcel vans from Weymouth Quay and was double-headed because it exceeded the weight limit for unassisted ascent of Upwey bank.

Chris Phillips

'West Country' class No. 34023 *Blackmore Vale* arrives at Weymouth with a Waterloo service shortly before the end of steam on the Southern Region. Fortunately, after withdrawal in July 1967, *Blackmore Vale* was sold to the Bluebell Railway, where she can be seen today.

Chris Phillips

The chalked message on the smokebox door – 'The End. The Last One' – needs little explanation. The last steam-hauled passenger train from Waterloo to Weymouth was the 8.30 a.m. service on Saturday 8 July 1967. 'Merchant Navy' class No. 35023 *Holland–Afrika Line* is seen at platform 5 on arrival at Weymouth. This was one of the two new platforms completed in 1957.

J.H. Lucking/Dorset County Museum

The original station building at Weymouth, seen here on 14 October 1965 after being freshly repaired and repainted. However, by the 1980s the remaining buildings were in a sorry state and the last part of the old station was replaced by a purpose-built building which opened in July 1986.

J.H. Lucking/Dorset County Museum

'West Country' class No. 34102 *Lapford* being 'oiled up' at Weymouth during 1965. The roof of the goods shed can be seen to the left. *Lapford* and *Blackmore Vale* were the last unrebuilt 'West Countries' in service, being withdrawn in July 1967.

Chris Phillips

BR Standard class 5s Nos 73041 and 73080 *Merlin* receive attention at Weymouth. No. 73041 was transferred from Eastleigh to Guildford in May 1965 and withdrawn the following month. No. 73080 was allocated to Weymouth shed until withdrawal in December 1966. This view also shows the line to Weymouth Quay on the right.

Chris Phillips

Great Western pannier tank No. 1367 proceeds along Commercial Road with a van train during 1956. Delays caused through the obstruction of the line by parked vehicles increased significantly in later years.

I.D. Beale

To comply with regulations, the flagman walks ahead of the train as No. 1368 leaves the quay with the Up Channel Islands boat train on 26 August 1961. Although scheduled passenger services ceased in 1987, a number of specials have visited the quay, and despite continuing uncertainty the line survives today.

Roy Panting

Weymouth Quay in 1956, with pannier tank No. 1370 engaged on shunting duties. The original quay building remained in use until 1965, when a new terminal was built. The limitations of the site resulted in frequent congestion, and in 1972 goods traffic ceased due to insufficient space to handle the developing container traffic.

I.D. Beale

Weymouth station in October 1956, five years after removal of the overall roof. On the right the land is being prepared for the new platforms. The massive two-road goods shed can be seen on the left. The goods yard closed in August 1972. This view was apparently taken from the tower of Christ Church in King Street, shortly before its demolition.

British Railways/Dorset County Museum

Melcombe Regis on the line to Portland closed in March 1952. However, to ease pressure at Weymouth on summer Saturdays, passenger trains regularly used the platform until September 1959 and occasionally thereafter. This view on 30 October 1965 shows the station largely intact, including the unusual windbreak opposite the main building.

J.H. Lucking/Dorset County Museum

The original Portland station was opened in 1865 but closed in 1902 after completion of the Easton and Church Hope line and the construction of a new station on the curve to Easton. This view taken on 31 October 1965 shows the old station which had remained in use as a goods office until April of that year. The building was later demolished to make way for a roundabout.

J.H. Lucking/Dorset County Museum

The interior of the original station at Portland on 3 June 1959, in use as a goods depot. Note also the elaborate construction of the timber roof.

J.H. Lucking/Dorset County Museum

The REC railtour of 7 June 1958 arrives at the derelict 'new' Portland station of 1902 on the curve to Easton. This station closed to passenger traffic in March 1952 but remained in use for goods until April 1965.

R.M. Casserley

Easton was the terminus of the Easton and Church Hope extension, opened initially for goods traffic only in 1900. However, passenger services commenced from 1 September 1902. This view shows Adams 02 class No. 30179 in the main platform and another unidentified member of the class taking on water from the GWR-style water tower. The last passenger services ran on 1 March 1952. Note the single-road engine shed on the far left.

Lens of Sutton

Another view of the REC railtour on 7 June 1958, seen here at Easton. By this time the engine shed and signal-box had been demolished and the platform railings removed.

R.M. Casserley

Pannier tank No. 9620 leaves Easton with a goods train. Although passenger services had been withdrawn in 1952, goods traffic continued until 5 April 1965.

Keith Hastie

This overall view of Upwey & Broadwey was taken in the 1950s after the station had been renamed following the closure of the Abbotsbury branch. The branch platform is on the left, and the line curving away down the 1 in 44 gradient towards Upwey station, pictured below.

I.D. Beale

Upwey was the first station on the Abbotsbury branch and was originally named Broadwey. Although the branch closed in 1952, freight services continued to operate to this station until 1 January 1962. This view, taken on 7 July 1961, shows the original station building, minus canopy, which is now part of industrial premises.

R.M. Casserley

The Great Western corrugated iron pagoda waiting shelter at Coryates Halt is seen here in 1952, shortly before closure of the branch.

I.D. Beale

A general view of Portesham station looking towards Abbotsbury. An old Camp Coach can be seen on the right. These were once a popular feature of the branch. The main building still survives today, having been converted into a private dwelling during 1963–64.

Lens of Sutton

Abbotsbury station in 1952, showing the first train of the day, comprising a Great Western 1400 class locomotive and auto-trailer. Several scenes in Powell & Pressburger's 1948 film *The Small Back Room* feature Abbotsbury station, when David Farrar, playing a bomb-disposal expert, comes down from London to defuse an experimental German bomb found on Chesil Bank.

I.D. Beale

Great Western 1400 class No. 1454 and auto-trailer stand at Abbotsbury station during the final years of the branch. The last train departed at 8.55 p.m. on Saturday 29 November 1952, with 1400 class No. 1453 propelling two auto-trailers. The station building was demolished in 1963 and a bungalow built on the site.

David Haysom Collection

Great Western Churchward 2800 class No. 2856 with a banked goods train passes Upwey Wishing Well Halt in 1959, two years after the station's closure. The concrete waiting shelter was removed shortly after, although the platforms remained intact until recent years. The two concrete stairways leading up from the main Dorchester–Weymouth road still survive today.

I.D. Beale

A general view of Dorchester West station looking towards Yeovil on 30 October 1965. Until 1934 the station had an overall roof and in later years the Up platform buildings were demolished. The signal-box in the distance was closed on 9 June 1968. The station, which remains open, was taken over by the Southern Region in 1950 and in November 1959 'West' was added to the nameboard.

J.H. Lucking/Dorset County Museum

The main building at Dorchester West on 30 October 1965. This is a fine example of Wilts, Somerset and Weymouth Railway architecture and was originally built in 1856. However, the station became unstaffed from January 1972 and the listed main building fell into increasing dereliction. Extensive renovation works commenced in 1990 and the building has been converted into the China Station restaurant!

J.H. Lucking/Dorset County Museum

Bradford Peverell & Stratton Halt looking south towards Dorchester. This halt opened in May 1933 and like other halts on the line was originally constructed of timber, but was rebuilt with precast concrete sectional platforms in 1959. However, although closed in October 1966, the platforms survive today and the halt may yet be reopened following the building of new housing in the area.

Lens of Sutton

Great Western Churchward 4300 class with an Up train at Grimstone & Frampton in 1959. The station opened with the line in 1857 and was initially named Frampton. The small goods yard to the left of this view closed on 1 May 1961.

I.D. Beale

In contrast, a DMU is seen at the Down platform on 5 April 1965. Staffing ceased in April 1966 and closure followed in October of that year. The buildings were demolished during 1967.

J.H. Lucking/Dorset County Museum

The station at Maiden Newton, seen here on 15 May 1965, looks little changed today. However, the lattice foot-bridge dating from the 1880s has been replaced with a redundant concrete structure from a closed station on the Salisbury–Exeter line.

J.H. Lucking/Dorset County Museum

Maiden Newton station looking south towards Dorchester on 15 May 1965. The covered wooden roof of the Bridport branch bay platform can be seen on the right. In the distance is the 56-lever signal-box built in 1921, which was taken out of use in 1988 but retained for use by the Permanent Way Department.

J.H. Lucking/Dorset County Museum

An unusual view from the covered Bridport branch platform. The cover was removed a few years before closure of the branch in May 1975.

Lens of Sutton

GWR Prairie No. 4562 seen at Maiden Newton in 1957 in the Bridport branch approach. Coaches in the gravity-shunt siding on the left are shown prior to gravitating into the branch bay.

I.D. Beale

A Great Western pannier tank on the Bridport branch, shortly after leaving Maiden Newton with a goods train in 1957.

I.D. Beale

Toller station on 22 January 1967 looking towards Maiden Newton. By this time the goods loop had been lifted, following withdrawal of freight services on 4 April 1960. This traffic had included watercress, and timber for pit props and sleepers.

Roy Panting

A single-car DMU approaches Powerstock in 1965. These had replaced two-car sets that year and continued to work the line until closure in 1975.

J.H. Lucking/Dorset County Museum

The station at Powerstock, originally built in 1857, was known briefly as Poorstock. This 1965 view shows the main building shortly before it was converted for residential use.

J.H. Lucking/Dorset County Museum

Bridport station was opened in 1857 and from 1887 to 1902 was known as Bradpole Road. 57XX class pannier tank No. 5781 prepares to depart with the branch train in August 1954. The 27-lever signal-box on the right was built in 1894 and closed on 8 June 1965.

I.D. Beale

The REC special of 7 June 1958 arrives at Bridport. This view looking north shows the additional dock siding added in 1909 on the left and the single-road engine shed. The small depot which was a sub-shed of Weymouth closed on 15 June 1959.

R.M. Casserley

Regular steam operation of the line ceased with the arrival of three-car DMUs in 1959. This view shows one of the first units at Bridport. From 1965 until closure in May 1975 the line was worked by single units. The station was unstaffed from October 1969. The last day of operation, Saturday 3 May 1975, saw a four-car unit in use, bringing enthusiasts from all parts of the country. Today no trace remains of the station, with commercial premises occupying the whole site.

I.D. Beale

Bridport East Street station closed to passengers in 1930, but survived in use as a private house for many years. This view looking towards the main station building was taken during the REC railtour of 7 June 1958.

R.M. Casserley

Pannier tank No. 3763 stands at West Bay station in August 1955. The line from Bridport had been closed to passenger traffic since September 1930. However, due to flooding caused by heavy rain, the line became the only means of transport to Bridport at the time of this photograph.

I.D. Beale

The REC special, with push-pull fitted M7 class No. 30107, arrives at West Bay on 7 June 1958. The station was remarkably intact nearly thirty years after closure to passenger traffic. The stone-built signal-box on the platform was closed in January 1927. The elevator on the far left was used for loading shingle.

R.M. Casserley

Limited goods traffic, mainly coal and shingle, continued to be handled at West Bay until December 1962. Track-lifting from the main station at Bridport took place in March 1965. The station site has been used as a boat yard in more recent years, with the station buildings remaining largely unaltered.

Lens of Sutton

The Lyme Regis branch, which opened in 1903, left the main line at Axminster. The village of Combpyne, with its famous viaduct, was the sole intermediate station. However, only Lyme Regis itself is actually in Dorset and this 1960s view shows in Ivatt tank approaching the station. The small LSWR signal-box seen here was closed on 20 July 1965, only four months before the branch closed.

Lens of Sutton

Adams Radial No. 30584 arrives at Lyme Regis with the branch train in May 1955. Following withdrawal in 1961, sister engine No. 30583 was preserved by the Bluebell Railway.

J.H. Lucking/Dorset County Museum

The mainstay of the branch services for nearly fifty years were the Adams Radial tanks. Despite unsuccessful attempts to replace these ageing locomotives with more modern motive power, the three surviving Radials continued to work the branch until the arrival of the Ivatt tanks in 1961.

Lens of Sutton

Ivatt class 2 tank No. 41308 stands at Lyme Regis station in August 1963, shortly before the end of regular steam operation. DMUs and single railcars operated the line until closure in November 1965.

Ken MacDonald

A general view of Lyme Regis station on 2 July 1965. The yard had closed in February 1964, and by the time of this photograph all the sidings had been removed and only the platform track remained. The wooden station building remained intact until 1979, when it was largely removed by the Mid-Hants Railway and added to the existing station building at Alresford.

J.H. Lucking/Dorset County Museum

Cattistock Halt, close to the village it served, was opened in 1931. It is seen here after rebuilding with precast concrete in 1959. However, the halt closed only seven years later and the sectional platforms were used to replace the wooden halts at Chetnole and Thornford Bridge further up the line towards Yeovil.

Lens of Sutton

No. 4914 *Cranmore Hall* at Evershot with a Weymouth service in 1959. The cattle dock can be seen on the left. Goods traffic was withdrawn in September 1964, with the station being closed on 3 October 1966 and demolished the following year.

I.D. Beale

Chetnole Halt, seen here in its original form, was opened in 1933. The staggered wooden platforms were situated either side of a roadbridge and were replaced after 1966 with one of the redundant concrete platforms from Cattistock. The halt remains open today, with trains stopping upon request to the guard.

Lens of Sutton

Yetminster opened with the line in 1857 to serve the adjoining village. The station remains open today, although it has been unstaffed since 1969. This view looking south towards Dorchester shows the station in happier days, before the majority of the buildings were demolished. The Down platform survives, although due to singling only the Up platform is still in use.

Lens of Sutton

This view of Thornford Bridge Halt was taken from under the roadbridge which separated the staggered wooden platforms, similar to those at Chetnole already described. This halt received the other concrete platform from Cattistock after the latter's closure in 1966. Thornford still remains open, although the village from which it takes its name is over a mile to the east.

Lens of Sutton

Yeovil Junction, on the main Salisbury–Exeter line, is just within the county of Dorset. This view on 17 October 1965 shows a Warship diesel and DMU at the main platform. In 1964 the station had been scheduled for closure following a scheme to create a railhead for east–west traffic at Sherborne. However, due to strong opposition the decision was reversed and the station remains open today, looking remarkably unchanged and even retaining a traditional buffet.

J.H. Lucking/Dorset County Museum

Warship diesel No. D829 *Magpie* stands in the Up platform at Sherborne during January 1967. Dieselization of the Western Region had taken place during 1965.

Chris Phillips

The only other station on the Salisbury–Exeter line within Dorset is Gillingham. This view looking towards Salisbury on 24 September 1965 shows a DMU service to Exeter Central. The next station to the west was Templecombe, which formed the junction with the Somerset and Dorset.

J.H. Lucking/Dorset County Museum

The much-lamented Somerset and Dorset Railway ran south from Bath Green Park to Bournemouth West. The first station within Dorset was Stalbridge and this interesting view shows the signal-box and level crossing gates which were once a common feature of British railways, though replaced extensively in recent years by automatic barriers.

Lens of Sutton

The tablet-catching apparatus at Stalbridge is demonstrated for the benefit of the photographers. Although the goods yard had closed in April 1965 and the points were disconnected three months later, the 18-lever signal-box remained in use to control the gates until closure of the S&D in March 1966. The line south of Blandford was however retained for goods traffic until January 1969.

Lens of Sutton

A general view of Sturminster Newton station looking south towards Blandford. In the foreground, the foot crossing on the Up platform retained a dropped edge which was a feature of early stations. The goods yard on the left closed on 5 April 1965, along with other stations on the Dorset section of the S&D, when freight handling was concentrated at Hendford, Yeovil.

Lens of Sutton

Shillingstone was a repeated winner of the Best-Kept Station Competition and is seen here on 21 September 1965 with BR Standard class 5 No. 73086 *The Green Knight*, minus nameplate and smokebox number, on the 9.00 a.m. Bristol–Bournemouth West through train. Unlike the other stations on the Dorset half of the S&D, the main building and platform canopy at Shillingstone survive intact today.

J.H. Lucking/Dorset County Museum

Blandford Forum station looking north in 1965. The 'Forum' suffix was added in 1953. Note the unusual signal-box which projected over the Down siding. After closure of the S&D in March 1966 the line to Blandford was retained for freight until 6 January 1969, when the yard finally closed. In common with other former stations in Dorset, the site has been redeveloped as a housing estate.

J.H. Lucking/Dorset County Museum

BR Standard 5 class No. 73051 leaves Bailey Gate station with an Up train around 1957. On the left behind the home signal can be seen the two boiler house chimneys of the milk depot, which has now been converted into small industrial units.

Colin Caddy Collection

BR Standard class 4 No. 76061 enters Bailey Gate with a Bournemouth West service in January 1966. This station was originally named Sturminster Marshall after the village it served, but was renamed when the line was extended to include a station at Sturminster Newton in 1863.

Colin Caddy Collection

This view looking south towards Corfe Mullen shows No. 73051 with an Up train around 1957. To the left is the entrance to the goods yard and the United Dairies sidings. The yard closed on 5 April 1965, in common with several other stations on the line.

Colin Caddy Collection

BR Standard class 4 tank No. 80043 departs from Bailey Gate in January 1963 with a train for Bournemouth West comprised of Midland Region stock.

Colin Caddy Collection

BR Standard class 4 tank No. 80134 passes Bailey Gate Crossing with a Down train around 1963. This signal-box was 1½ miles from Bailey Gate station and controlled the busy crossing on the A31 Wimborne to Bere Regis road. The brick base of the box still survives today.

J.W.T. House/Colin Caddy Collection

'West Country' class No. 34041 *Wilton* with an Up train at Bailey Gate Crossing around 1963. The crossing keeper's cottage to the right of the signal-box is still occupied.

Colin Caddy Collection

BR Standard class 4 No. 75073 at Corfe Mullen with the 3.40 p.m. Bournemouth West–Bath service in July 1964.

Colin Caddy Collection

BR Standard class 4 No. 75072 passes Corfe Mullen signal-box on the single line to Broadstone with a Down train in 1957. The signal-box has been demolished but surprisingly the crossing gates still survive. On the right is the original route from Wimborne which was closed to passenger traffic in 1920 and goods from 1933. Only the mile-long section from Corfe Mullen to Carter's clay siding was retained, which was shunted by Down goods trains until September 1959.

Colin Caddy Collection

A general view of Wimborne station looking south towards Broadstone. Wimborne originally opened with the completion of the Southampton–Dorchester line in 1847. This indirect and tortuous route became known as 'Castleman's Corkscrew' after a promoter of the line who was a solicitor at Wimborne. No doubt operational difficulties were caused at this once-busy junction station by the 30-chain curve apparent in this view. The station closed with the Broadstone–Brockenhurst line on 4 May 1964.

David Haysom Collection

Push-pull fitted M7 class No. 30480 in the Up platform at Wimborne during 1963. The base of the unique tall brick-built signal-box can also be seen.

Chris Phillips

The interior of the 29-lever box at Wimborne in 1963, with signalman George Fenemore posing obligingly for the photographer. Note the various block instruments, signal repeaters and brass bell plungers. This box was reduced to a ground frame in 1966 and finally closed on 8 January 1967.

Chris Phillips

Unrebuilt 'Battle of Britain' class No. 34063 *229 Squadron* at Wimborne with a Bournemouth West–Salisbury train in 1963. The unusual signal-box is seen to advantage in this view.

Stan Symes

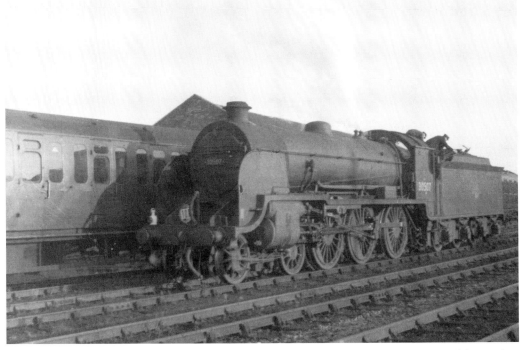

A Urie S15 at Wimborne in 1963. The crew are pulling forward the coal from the rear of the tender. This locomotive was withdrawn in December 1963. The large goods shed can be seen behind, and local goods traffic was to continue until May 1977.

Chris Phillips

Q class No. 30548 arrives at Wimborne with push-pull set No. 33 on a Brockenhurst–Bournemouth West service in 1959. Set No. 33 was formed in 1939 and withdrawn in January 1960. No. 30548 was possibly substituting for a failed M7. Note the ornate LSWR swan-neck gas lamp on the left.

Ken MacDonald

Maunsell Q class No. 30546 enters West Moors station from Wimborne with a Bournemouth West–Brockenhurst service on 14 April 1964.

Allen White

An M7 and two-coach push-pull set arrive from Brockenhurst with a Bournemouth West service. This set was withdrawn in November 1958. On the left is the junction of the line to Salisbury which closed on 4 May 1964. The goods yard at West Moors also closed on that day, although traffic to the Army Petrol Depot continued until 1974. Goods traffic to Ringwood ceased in August 1967.

David Haysom Collection

An unidentified Q class locomotive departs from West Moors on 1 April 1964. Maunsell push-pull set No. 604 was one of the last to be withdrawn in November of that year.

Allen White

Verwood station on 30 April 1964, less than a week before closure of the Salisbury–West Moors line. BR Standard class 4 No. 75065 is seen entering the Down platform with a goods from Salisbury. Only the roadbridge and the Albion Hotel survive at this location today.

Allen White

BR Standard class 4 No. 76062 passes Daggons Road station with a goods from Salisbury on 10 April 1964. Since closure of the line the signal-box and the adjacent road have been removed but the station building remains as a private dwelling.

Allen White

Returning to the 'old road', BR Standard class 4 No. 76009 is seen standing at Wimborne station with a service from Brockenhurst in 1963. The 'Up Poole Siding' on the left remained in use until 1965.

Chris Phillips

Maunsell U class No. 31623 crosses the River Stour on the approach to Wimborne with the 1.03 p.m. Bournemouth West–Salisbury train on 30 April 1964.

Roy Panting

Broadstone was the junction for the Somerset and Dorset. This view looking north on 13 August 1965 shows the large junction station at which passengers between Bournemouth and Weymouth had to change until the direct route via Poole was opened with the completion of the Holes Bay curve in 1893. The Hamworthy Junction line on the left lost its passenger services on 4 May 1964.

J.H. Lucking/Dorset County Museum

Drummond T9 class No. 30718 arrives at platform 4 with a RCTS special on an extremely wet day. This locomotive was eventually withdrawn in March 1961. Passenger services to Broadstone ceased with the closure of the Somerset and Dorset in March 1966. However, the signal-box remained in use, with the retention of the line to Blandford for goods traffic, until October 1970. A single track to Wimborne remained in use until May 1977.

Keith Hastie

Push-pull fitted M7 class No. 30104 leaves Broadstone with a Brockenhurst–Bournemouth West service on 18 July 1960. The headcode displayed is in fact for Brockenhurst–Lymington services, but in later years this system of route indication was not always strictly followed.

H.C. Casserley

Creekmoor Halt looking towards Poole on 24 September 1965. This halt opened in June 1933 and unlike many similar halts included a concrete overbridge.

J.H. Lucking/Dorset County Museum

A Bath–Bournemouth West service arrives at Creekmoor Halt on 8 August 1962. BR Standard class 4 No. 75027 is now preserved on the Bluebell Railway. Creekmoor also closed with the Somerset and Dorset line in March 1966.

R.M. Casserley

After leaving Creekmoor, BR Standard class 4 No. 76025 approaches Holes Bay Junction with the 12.08 p.m. Brockenhurst–Bournemouth West train on 19 April 1964.

Roy Panting

BR Standard class 4 No. 75003, hauling Bulleid three-coach set No. 781, leaves Holes Bay Junction with a Bournemouth West–Salisbury service on 19 April 1964. The main line to Weymouth on the Holes Bay curve can be seen in the distance, with the familiar twin chimneys of Poole power station beyond. At the time of writing these had just been demolished.

Roy Panting

The LCGB 'Hampshire Venturer Rail Tour', hauled by Q class No. 30548, returns to the main Bournemouth–Weymouth line at Holes Bay Junction on 19 April 1964.

Roy Panting

The Swanage Branch

A general view from the foot-bridge of Wareham station looking west towards Weymouth during the late 1950s. M7 class No. 30128 awaits departure to Swanage with a local train from Bournemouth West. The push-pull set is one of the LSWR ironclad sets numbered 381–5 which were converted to push-pull use in 1949. In the Up bay, M7 class No. 30108 waits, having arrived earlier from Swanage.

David Haysom Collection

BR Standard class 4 tank No. 80146 awaits departure to Swanage from the Down bay during the summer of 1964. These locomotives, together with the Ivatt class 2 tanks and BR class 3 tanks, replaced the M7s in May 1964. The Maunsell push–pull sets lasted until the end of 1964.

Chris Phillips

'Merchant Navy' class No. 35022 *Holland–America Line* prepares to continue its journey to Weymouth during the summer of 1964. Ivatt tank No. 41312 waits in the Down bay with a Swanage train.

Chris Phillips

Ivatt tank No. 41312 with Maunsell push-pull set No. 610 is seen in close-up. No. 41312 was originally based in Kent, then came to Bournemouth for a short while before ending its days at Nine Elms on empty carriage workings. It was finally withdrawn in July 1967.

Chris Phillips

A good view of M7 class No. 30107, a Swanage branch regular until withdrawal, in the Down bay at Wareham. Although frowned upon by the authorities, the practice of carrying both route indicator disc and tail lamps was common.

Chris Phillips

Fireman Ken Hordle replenishes the tanks of an Ivatt class 2 locomotive from the water column at the west end of Wareham Down platform. The water tower can be seen in the background. It was built with the 'new' Wareham station in 1886 and supplied water to both Up and Down platform water columns.

Stan Symes

LSWR push-pull set No. 36 is seen to good advantage converging with the main line at Worgret Junction, having travelled the length of the Swanage branch. The motive power was as usual supplied by a Bournemouth-based M7. The coaches were formed into push-pull sets in 1939 and set No. 36 was finally withdrawn in May 1959, although the brake coach was replaced in October 1956.

R.R. Bowler

Worgret Junction signal-box was situated at the point of divergence of the Swanage branch from the main Bournemouth–Weymouth line. It opened with the branch in 1885 and finally closed on 23 May 1976. The tablet-catching apparatus for the branch can be seen to good effect. The box was replaced with a 5-lever ground frame which controlled access to Furzebrook sidings. These continue to provide revenue for the railway with block trains of liquified petroleum gas.

Tony Trood

The 16-lever frame and assorted block instruments can be seen clearly, together with the track diagram, in this fine interior shot of Worgret box on 23 June 1968. The immaculate condition is apparent and it is obvious that the signalmen took pride in their job.

Tony Trood

Ivatt tank No. 41224, having passed under Holme Lane bridge, starts to descend towards the River Frome flood plain before the climb to Worgret. This locomotive was originally allocated to the Midland Region and was in fact push-pull fitted before its arrival at Bournemouth. The train consists of two Bulleid corridor coaches.

Chris Phillips

'West Country' class No. 34004 *Yeovil* climbs towards Holme Lane bridge and Furzebrook. The train ran on 11 June 1967 and, as the headboard indicates, was on a LSWR 'Farewell to Steam' railtour which originated in Birmingham.

Roy Panting

The four-arch viaduct built of local Purbeck stone is seen during the late 1950s with an unidentified M7, push-pull set No. 1, and through coaches for Waterloo at the rear.

Ken MacDonald

BR Standard class 3 tank No. 82028 heads towards the viaduct from Corfe with the 2.45 p.m. Swanage–Wareham train on 19 April 1964. This locomotive stayed at Bournemouth shed for only eight months before being sent to Nine Elms. It was withdrawn in September 1966 and unfortunately none of this type has been spared for preservation.

Roy Panting

Towards the end of steam, diesels appeared more regularly on the branch. A green-liveried Crompton on a Waterloo–Swanage express heads towards Corfe station through Challow Hill cutting and past the lofty LSWR home signal. This signal, together with the one in the foreground, remain in place today.

Bryan Green

Ivatt tank No. 41238 arrives at Corfe with a Maunsell set for Swanage during the summer of 1964. This locomotive was based for most of its life at Nuneaton on the Midland Region, was later transferred to Bournemouth in the early 1960s and was withdrawn in April 1965.

Stan Symes

An overall view of Corfe Castle station taken on 31 August 1966. The station was solidly constructed of Purbeck stone, as were the majority of buildings and bridges on the line south of Corfe viaduct. It opened with the line in 1885 and remained largely unaltered, with the exception of the enlarging of the porters' lobby to form a new signal-box in 1956. The original signal-box stood next to the waiting shelter on the Down platform. The new box closed officially with the line on 3 January 1972. In the background are the Pullman Camping Coaches.

Roy Panting

M7 class No. 30107 waits for departure with an ironclad push-pull set at Corfe Castle Down platform. Although the locomotive was fitted with the automatic warning system, as witnessed by the battery underneath the bunker, it was only partially complete and never operated. This view was taken on 7 July 1962.

Roy Panting

Ivatt tank No. 41230, seen in the Up platform in July 1966, stands in readiness for the arrival of the Down service which will cross here. The importance to the branch of holiday traffic can be gauged by the large number of passengers waiting for the Swanage train. No. 41230 spent most of its working life in Wales and was withdrawn from Bournemouth shed in April 1967.

Roy Panting

Towards the end of steam various special trains traversed the branch. 'West Country' class No. 34023 *Blackmore Vale* passes through Corfe station on 7 May 1967 with the 'Dorset Coast Express' bound for Swanage. During 1966–67 many named locomotives had their plates removed for 'safekeeping', as they were rapidly becoming collectors' items. The castle provides an impressive backdrop to the scene.

Roy Panting

Former Pullman car No. P43 provided holiday accommodation in the goods yard at Corfe. Mains services were supplied. BR later decided that this seasonal operation was uneconomic and holiday coaches became a thing of the past. This coach was cut up and burnt on site during 1968.

Keith Hastie

Ivatt tank No. 41303, with a Maunsell push–pull set, is viewed from the cab of another Ivatt tank. The trains are crossing at Corfe during the summer of 1964. No. 41303, with its smokebox number obscured, carries a new 70F, formerly 71B, Bournemouth shed plate and shows the narrow chimney designed by Swindon to good effect. This locomotive was withdrawn in September 1964.

Stan Symes

M7 class No. 30111, with driver Johnny Spicer looking out, enters Corfe Up platform around 1960. Its train consists of an ironclad push–pull set and through coaches to Waterloo. In the Down platform a train of well-patronized Maunsell coaches awaits a clear section to Swanage. No. 30111 was a regular locomotive on the Swanage branch and was withdrawn from Bournemouth shed in January 1964, shortly before all push–pull working ceased.

Keith Hastie

Corfe Castle and station viewed from the driver's cab of a three-car Hampshire unit in the late 1960s. Goods facilities were withdrawn from the station in September 1965 and the yard points were clipped and padlocked. In the foreground, the LSWR lattice-built home signal is prominent. The loop at Corfe was extended towards Swanage in December 1943 to accommodate trains of increased length.

Chris Phillips

Drummond 700 class No. 30695 approaches Victoria Avenue bridge with the 9.24 a.m. ex-Swanage service in August 1953. It was unusual for a member of this class to be seen on a passenger working, although during the summer months a shortage of locomotives often made this necessary. The stock comprises an ex-LSWR three-coach set and later Maunsell carriages.

R.R. Bowler

BR Standard class 4 No. 75079, viewed from the advance starter, heads up the gradient towards Corfe on a through train to Eastleigh in September 1965. The locomotive has a large tender of 4725 gallons water capacity and a Brighton-designed double chimney. These particular engines were highly regarded by the Southern Region crews, especially those with large tenders. No. 75079 was shedded at Eastleigh and withdrawn in November 1966.

Chris Phillips

'West Country' class No. 34023 *Blackmore Vale* slips spectacularly on departure with a twelve-coach Ramblers' excursion on a summer Sunday. Owing to its length, the train had to be flagged away from the station.

Chris Phillips

M7 class No. 30667 performs a small exercise in demolition as a result of a broken regulator link. The 50 ft turntable fell into disuse and was later cut up. Fortunately for the Swanage Railway, an exact replacement from Neasden London Transport depot was acquired and can be seen in use today.

Chris Phillips

Another M7, No. 30107, has a mishap at Swanage. The locomotive has derailed on the engine shed points under Northbrook Road bridge. The crew are busily assessing the damage!

Chris Phillips

A fine study of M7 class No. 30107 over the ash pit, with Swanage driver Johnny Spicer going about his daily routine. The larger number of pipes on the buffer beam and the vacuum cylinder below, together with the Westinghouse pump to the left of the smokebox, form part of the push–pull apparatus.

Chris Phillips

Viewed from the signal-box, an M7 proceeds towards the main platform, having received attention at the shed. Swanage shed was a sub-shed of Bournemouth.

Chris Phillips

A fine study of Swanage signalman Arthur Galton at work. Arthur's father Harry had also been a signalman at Swanage. After closure of the box on 6 June 1967 Arthur was transferred to Corfe Castle and worked there with Bob Richards until the branch closed in January 1972.

Chris Phillips

With steam leaking profusely, M7 class No. 30107 looks a sad sight. This locomotive was the last M7 to work the Swanage branch and was withdrawn from service the following day in May 1964.

Chris Phillips

During 1963 Crompton diesel No. D6578 was sent to Swanage on crew training. It is seen here in the run-round loop while an M7 and push-pull set await departure to Wareham from the bay.

Chris Phillips

BR Standard class 4 No. 76010 heads under Northbrook Road bridge with a branch train consisting of two Bulleid corridor coaches. The fireman prepares to hand the single-line tablet over to the Swanage signalman. Goods services were withdrawn in October 1965 and the line to the goods shed and two other sidings were lifted. Two roads were left intact for stock berthing.

Chris Phillips

BR Standard class 4 No. 76011 arrives tender-first with through coaches from the Midlands. This service ran for one summer season only via the S&D. The locomotive was shedded at Bournemouth and lasted until the end of steam in July 1967.

Chris Phillips

Swanage signalman Jimmy Hunt prepares to receive the single-line tablet from the fireman of a Standard 4 locomotive. The stock consists of a pair of Mk1 coaches. The single white disc above the centre of the buffer beam was Southern Region code number 4, used by all Swanage branch trains.

Chris Phillips

Swanage signalman Jimmy Hunt poses for the camera on the balcony of Swanage signal-box in July 1965. This box with a base of Purbeck stone opened with the branch in 1885 and contained a 23-lever Stevens-pattern frame. It closed on 6 June 1967.

Chris Phillips

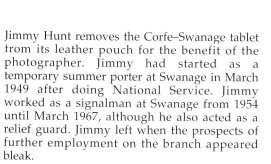

Jimmy Hunt removes the Corfe–Swanage tablet from its leather pouch for the benefit of the photographer. Jimmy had started as a temporary summer porter at Swanage in March 1949 after doing National Service. Jimmy worked as a signalman at Swanage from 1954 until March 1967, although he also acted as a relief guard. Jimmy left when the prospects of further employment on the branch appeared bleak.

Chris Phillips

The interior of Swanage signal-box is seen to advantage in this view. The tablet machine can just be glimpsed in the far corner, while above the frame the block shelf and track diagram complete the picture.

Chris Phillips

BR Standard class 4 tank No. 80085 heads a through working towards the main platform during the summer of 1966. Signalman Arthur Galton prepares to receive the tablet from the fireman. The leading coach is of Eastern Region origin and was designed by Thompson. Note the signalman's mode of transport.

Chris Phillips

Signalman Jimmy Hunt proceeds back to the box with the tablet from the fireman of BR Standard class 4 tank No. 80019. The train consists of Bulleid coaching stock and the locomotive was withdrawn from service in March 1967. The Southern Region offset gantry signal was the starting signal for the bay and came into use in the late 1950s when the LSWR bracket signal, situated on the main platform, was replaced by two separate signals.

Chris Phillips

A close-up of the tablet in its large pouch changing hands. No. 80032, having run round its train, proceeds back towards the main platform with the tablet in the safe hands of the fireman.

Chris Phillips

Ivatt tank No. 41312 waits in the bay with a Maunsell push-pull set bound for Wareham during the summer of 1964. This locomotive spent most of its working life in Kent and ended its days shunting stock at Waterloo and Clapham.

Chris Phillips

BR Standard Mogul No. 76013 heads past the signal-box with a branch train to Wareham during the summer of 1966. The engine lacks both smokebox numberplate and shed plate, and lasted only until September of that year.

Chris Phillips

The concentration shows in this study of signalman Bob Inman, who had started at Swanage as a summer porter in 1958. Bob was a signalman at both Swanage and Corfe. He left the railway in March 1967 at the same time as fellow signalman Jimmy Hunt.

Chris Phillips

132

BR Standard Mogul No. 76062 eases towards the stop blocks with a summer Sundays only excursion comprised of Bulleid stock from Eastleigh.

Chris Phillips

BR Standard Class 3 No. 82027 and a Maunsell push-pull set wait for departure to Wareham in the summer of 1964. This locomotive, together with sisters Nos 82026, 82028 and 82029, worked the summer branch services in harness with Ivatt tanks following withdrawal of the M7s in May 1964.

Chris Phillips

A general view of the station buildings and main approach taken in the mid-1960s. The station was originally of much smaller proportions and similar in size to Corfe. It was significantly extended in 1938 to cater for the increasing holiday traffic. The Benn and Cronin indicator board in the foreground gave a summary of train times and destinations.

Chris Phillips

Jack Cannons, station foreman at Swanage from 1963 until October 1969, proceeds towards the main station building from the goods office. Although goods facilities had been withdrawn, BR still provided a parcels delivery service, as witnessed by the delivery van in BR colours. The goods shed was built in 1885 and was virtually doubled in size in 1898. It closed officially in December 1965 and is now currently used by the Carriage and Wagon Department of the Swanage Railway.

Chris Phillips

Some of the station staff at Swanage pose outside the parcels office in the summer of 1965. Left to right: porter/shunter George Sims, porter/shunter Tom Titley, signalman Arthur Galton, station foreman Jack Cannons, porter Billy Hazell, and shunter/porter Bob Richards, who later, as a signalman, worked the final shift at Corfe Castle on 1 January 1972. Bob now works as a signalman at Wareham.

Chris Phillips

Two of the line's characters, porter/shunter George Sims (left) and porter Bill 'Taffy' Hazell, are seen outside the parcels office in 1966 wearing their new BR uniforms. 'Taffy' had started his career at Eastleigh Works in 1942 and came to Swanage as a porter in 1952. He left the railway on its closure in January 1972 and has continued to spend his retirement in Swanage.

Chris Phillips

135

The interior of the parcels office in 1966. On the far left is porter 'Taffy' Hazell with porter/shunter Ernie Farwell to his right, while on the opposite side of the office, porter George Sims is also seen at work. The gas lighting remained in use until the closure of the station.

Chris Phillips

Booking office clerk Bryan Green on duty at Swanage in 1965. Bryan joined the railway straight from school in September 1953 and initially helped out in the goods office at Swanage. He later spent two years in the enquiries office at Bournemouth Central after doing his National Service. Bryan returned to Swanage station in the early 1960s, where he shared the booking office shifts with Maurice Walton. This followed a period of relief work at Blandford, West Moors and other stations in the area. Bryan also left the railway in 1967 when the future of the line was in serious doubt.

Chris Phillips

A general view of the main platform in 1966, with porter/shunter Ernie Farwell sweeping up at the end of another day. Ernie had worked in the goods shed until the withdrawal of goods traffic in October 1965, when he became a porter. After the line closed he worked at Hayters, the local building firm. Since retiring he has much enjoyed the return of steam to Swanage. The station remains little changed apart from the clock seen here and the removal of the advert hoarding in the distance.

Chris Phillips

Porter/shunter George Sims, wearing his new uniform, collects tickets as passengers leave the station during 1966. George retired when the branch finally closed in 1972.

Chris Phillips

Bournemouth driver Stan Symes is seen topping up the lubricator on the Walschaerts valve gear of 'West Country' class No. 34024 *Tamar Valley*. The unusual cap originated in North America and was worn by Stan following a short spell working in Canada on the Canadian National and Canadian Pacific railways during 1952. Today Stan can still be found driving steam locomotives at Swanage as a volunteer.

Chris Phillips

In the final summer of steam operation, driver Jock Habgood and guard Alec Dudley are seen checking train details. BR Standard class 4 No. 76014, based at Bournemouth, was working the branch. This locomotive had only a few months' service left before it was withdrawn in September 1966.

Chris Phillips

Driver Stan Symes, on the left, guard Peter Buglar and fireman Doug Robinson pass the time of day while waiting to work an express service to Waterloo. 'West Country' class No. 34024 *Tamar Valley*, lacking nameplates and looking rather grubby, was rebuilt only five years previously in February 1961. She was shedded at Bournemouth and was finally withdrawn in July 1967.

Chris Phillips

A model-like scene as 'West Country' class No. 34040 *Crewkerne*, in immaculate condition at the head of an express to Waterloo, poses for the cameraman in the summer of 1966. Built at Brighton Works in September 1946, she was rebuilt in October 1960 and finally withdrawn from service at the end of steam.

Chris Phillips

'West Country' class No. 34023 *Blackmore Vale* in charge of a twelve-coach Ramblers' excursion. The starting signal cannot be pulled off as the train is standing past it and completing the track circuit. The signalman will therefore use a green flag to authorize departure.

Chris Phillips

The Bournemouth crew of an Ivatt tank locomotive hold up a boot to show the photographer the shape of things to come, as the locomotive runs round its stock. In the last years of steam on the Swanage branch, BR Standard class 4 2–6–0s and 2–6–4s largely replaced the smaller Ivatt locomotives.

Chris Phillips

An interesting view looking towards the main platform from the signal-box in the last years of steam operation. A BR Standard class 4 waits by the main platform with a through train to Eastleigh.

Chris Phillips

A BR Standard class 4 heads for Wareham with a branch train consisting of two Bulleid coaches, while a Brush Type 4 diesel waits at the main platform with a Sundays only return excursion working, during the summer of 1966. This train had to be flagged away on departure because it was forward of the main starting signal.

Chris Phillips

Following the withdrawal of steam on 4 September 1966 three-car Hampshire units were drafted in to run the branch services. Unit No. 1127 in green livery, seen here passing the signal-box, was one of the first of these units to be seen at Swanage.

Chris Phillips

Only three years after closure, this was all that remained of Swanage station on 12 September 1975. The track had been swiftly removed and the main station buildings allowed to become derelict. The main platform had been bulldozed up to the station canopy and the adjoining trackbed infilled to platform level. The colourful pedalos lined up beside the goods shed had just been removed from the beach at the end of the summer season. Although the Swanage Railway Society had been fighting against strong opposition to obtain permission to restore the railway since 1972, access to the main buildings was not finally granted until February 1976.

George Moon

Fifteen years later, the view from the same point is very different. 'Battle of Britain' class No. 34072 *257 Squadron* leaves the main platform at Swanage for Harmans Cross with a 'Santa Special' during December 1990. Through the determined efforts of the members of the Swanage Railway Project, steam still lives on in Dorset a generation after withdrawal from main-line operation. No. 34072 spent many years at Barry scrapyard before being restored to full running order in less than two years. Local railway photographer Chris Phillips, whose work in the 1960s comprises the Swanage section of this book, still continues to photograph steam on the branch today.

Chris Phillips

The weekend of 20/21 March 1993 found 'West Country' class No. 34105 *Swanage* at Swanage! This locomotive was in fact on short-term loan from the Mid-Hants Railway at Alresford. In the main platform, M7 class No. 30053 departs with a Harmans Cross service. No. 30053 was repatriated from the United States in 1987 and is now based at Swanage. Apart from the Great Western-style water tower, the 'Bournemouth Belle' headboard and the camcorders this could easily be a scene from the 1950s.

David Haysom Collection

A unique view of 'West Country' class No. 34105 *Swanage* at Swanage station on Sunday 21 March 1993, complete with the original enamel shield. This was based on the seal of the Swanage Urban District Council but was never carried in service. The shield had in fact been manufactured in 1946, when a locomotive carrying the name *Swanage* was originally scheduled to be built. However, as most of the order was to be allocated away from the West Country, 'Battle of Britain' names were substituted. *Swanage* was eventually numbered 34105 and built in March 1950. By this time the practice of naming the 'West Countries' at or near the actual towns had also ceased following Nationalization. The last so-named was No. 34091 *Weymouth* on 29 December 1949.

David Haysom Collection